I Think I Will Just Be Me

KAREN MOORE

PAGE PUBLISHING, INC.
Conneaut Lake, PA

First originally published by Page Publishing 2020

ISBN 978-1-6624-2426-7 (pbk)
ISBN 978-1-6624-2427-4 (digital)

Printed in the United States of America

To Brennan

If I were a rooster, I would get up really early and crow loud to wake you up every morning.

I don't like to get up early!

If I were a giraffe, I would have a long neck and eat leaves from a tree.

I wonder how many leaves I would have to eat to be full.

If I were a squirrel, I would hide nuts in an old tree and use my teeth to open them.

I might get a toothache!

If I were a baby deer, I would play in
the grass and run in the woods.

I hope I don't get lost!

If I were a pig, I would play in the mud.

I can't do that. I would have to take a lot of baths!

If I were a fish, I would live in the lake.

People would try to catch me with a hook.

Ouch! That would hurt me!

If I were a frog, I would play on a lily pad and eat bugs that I catch.

Yuck! I don't want to eat bugs.

If I were a snake, I would hide in the grass,
and I might scare people as they go by.

It's not funny to scare people!

If I were a rabbit, I would eat the lettuce in your garden.

Oh my! I might get chased by a big dog!

If I were a bird, I would sit in my nest and eat worms.

I wonder if I would like worms.

If I were a monkey, I would hang upside down in a tree and eat bananas.

I would probably fall on my head!

If I were a duck, I would fly high in
the sky with the puffy clouds!

I would be a long way from home!

I THINK I WILL
JUST BE ME!

My name is

_____

A spot for your name and picture to personalize.
Please tape or glue a picture of your child here.

┌──────────────┐
│   │
│   │
│   │
│   │
│   │
└──────────────┘

I THINK I WILL JUST BE ME.

CPSIA information can be obtained
at www.ICGtesting.com
Printed in the USA
LVHW071119030221
678222LV00007B/801